D0488844

CHC

**This book is to be returned on or before
the last date stamped below.**

1 2 MAR 2002	1 0 MAR 2007	
1 0 MAY 2002	2 5 APR 2007	
2 2 MAR 2003	16 May 2007	
2 3 MAY 2003	- 1 APR 2008	
2 4 JUN 2003	1 8 JAN 2011	
1 9 JUN 2004		
2 1 JUN 2005		
3 MAY 2006		
- 8 NOV 2006		

**LEARNING FOR LIFE
LONDON BOROUGH OF SUTTON LIBRARIES**

RENEWALS   Please quote: date of return, your ticket number
and computer label number for each item.

Oxford University Press, Great Clarendon Street, Oxford OX2 6DP

Oxford   New York
Athens   Auckland   Bangkok   Bogotá   Bombay
Buenos Aires   Calcutta   Cape Town   Dar es Salaam
Delhi   Florence   Hong Kong   Istanbul   Karachi
Kuala Lumpur   Madras   Madrid   Melbourne
Mexico City   Nairobi   Paris   Singapore
Taipei   Tokyo   Toronto   Warsaw

and associated companies in
Berlin   Ibadan

Oxford is a trade mark of Oxford University Press

Text © Pratima Mitchell 1997
Illustrations © Oxford University Press 1997

A CIP catalogue record for this book is available from the British Library

ISBN 0-19-910436-0 (hardback)
0-19-910442-5 (paperback)
0-19-918654-5 (Branch Library Pack B)
3 5 7 9 10 8 6 4

Printed in Hong Kong

Gandhi

THE FATHER OF MODERN INDIA

PRATIMA MITCHELL

Illustrated by Mrinal Mitra

OXFORD UNIVERSITY PRESS

Mohandas Karamchand Gandhi was small, shy and not very clever at school. Who would have guessed that one day he would free India from British rule?

Mohandas was born on October 2 1869, in the small town of Porbander, north of Bombay. At that time, India was part of the British Empire. Queen Victoria was not only Queen of England, but also Empress of India, with its millions of people and many different religions. Indian people felt helpless because they had no power in their own country.

Mohandas's family was traditional Hindu, but his father had friends from all religions. He was taught to respect the beliefs of others, and was brought up in an atmosphere of love and trust. One day he stole a small piece of gold from his brother. He never forgot the expression of love and forgiveness on his father's face when he confessed to him.

When Mohandas was thirteen, his parents chose a wife for him. Her name was Kasturba. Like all children, they squabbled and sulked at first, but later they became great friends.

Mohandas went to England when he was seventeen, to study to become a lawyer. The journey took three long weeks by ship. Mohandas was very shy and unsure of himself. At meal times he stayed in his cabin and ate the fruit and sweets that his relatives had given him.

England felt so cold and strange. He felt lonely, but he knew he must learn to be more sociable. He joined a ballroom dancing class and started taking violin lessons. With a smart new jacket, striped trousers and a top hat he thought he could be a young man about town in London, the centre of the British Empire, the greatest power in the world.

But trying to become a "brown Englishman" felt unnatural; instead, Mohandas started to read the Gita, a very important book for Hindus, and the Bible. He day-dreamed about home and missed his mother.

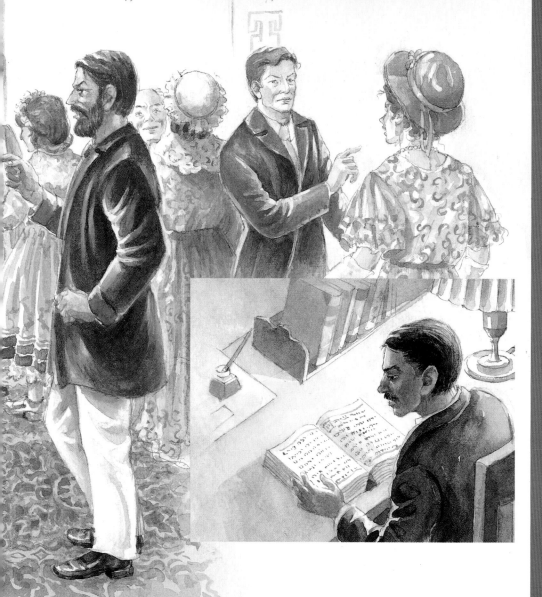

After three years in England, Mohandas qualified as a lawyer. He returned to his home town. Sadly, his mother had died, but waiting for him was Kasturba and their baby son, Harilal. Work was hard to find in India, so in 1893 Mohandas accepted a job in South Africa.

In those days South Africa was also part of the British Empire. The British brought in thousands of workers from India and other parts of Asia for their farms and factories. Mohandas was shocked to find that the workers were treated like slaves.

One day, Mohandas bought a first class train ticket to Pretoria. He made himself comfortable for the journey, but a white passenger rudely told him to move to another carriage. When Mohandas refused, the guard pushed him off the train.

This incident made a deep impression on Mohandas. He sat all night in a freezing cold waiting room, thinking. Why shouldn't brown and black people have the same rights as the whites? "They treat us like beasts", he told a friend, and made up his mind to help the Asians to stand up for themselves.

Mohandas returned to India to fetch his family, and South Africa became their home for the next twenty years.

In 1899 war broke out in South Africa between the British and the Dutch. Both countries wanted to control the diamond mines, gold fields and rich farmland.

Although Mohandas believed that violence or war was never a solution to any quarrel, he still thought that the Indians should be loyal to the British.

To the great amazement of the British, Mohandas organised an Indian Ambulance Service to take part in the Boer War. He and his volunteers ran on to the battlefields, risking their own lives to carry wounded British soldiers to safety on stretchers.

Despite this, once the war was over and the British and the Dutch became friends again, the Asians were treated worse than before. But Mohandas did not lose heart. He continued to urge the Asian people in South Africa to stand up for themselves.

Mohandas was loved and admired as a politician because he had a unique message. He explained that standing up for what is right and true should never lead to anger or violence. He called this way of behaving Satyagraha, which means Truth Force. His followers called him Gandhibhai – brother Gandhi. He taught the Asians that they deserved respect and should speak up against unfair laws.

In 1906 he organised a huge meeting for Asians in South Africa – Hindus, Muslims and Christians. They all vowed that they would never again obey South Africa's unfair laws, which did not even allow them to walk on the same pavements as white people.

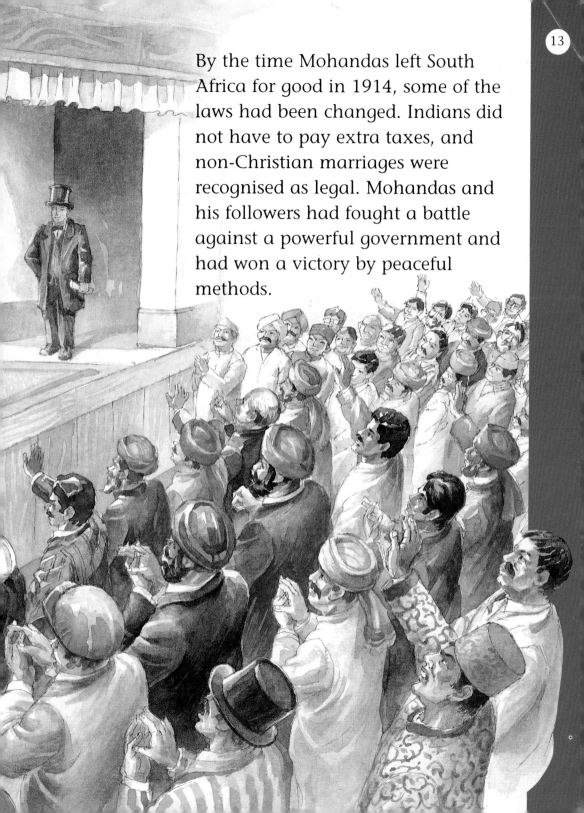

By the time Mohandas left South Africa for good in 1914, some of the laws had been changed. Indians did not have to pay extra taxes, and non-Christian marriages were recognised as legal. Mohandas and his followers had fought a battle against a powerful government and had won a victory by peaceful methods.

Word had reached India about the remarkable Satyagraha movement, and when Mohandas returned in 1914, thousands of people were there to welcome him. The great poet, Rabindranath Tagore, gave him another name – Mahatma, which means "Great Soul".

Indians had organised their own political party, called the Indian National Congress. The Congress party was demanding the chance for Indians to run their own country. But Mohandas wanted more than political power for Indians. He wanted them to become more Indian in their ways, to learn their own languages, dress in Indian clothes, live simply and help with the problems of poor farmers.

He set an example by forming a community called Sabarmati Ashram. His home was a hut, and he wore the cotton *dhoti* of a peasant. He ate sparingly, and wrote down his thoughts to share with people throughout India. Every day he spun yarn at his spinning wheel.

He even cleaned out the toilets in the Ashram. This was the work of the lowest class, who used to be called the "untouchables". But Mohandas renamed them "Harijans", which means "children of God". He welcomed a Harijan family into the Ashram and adopted their little daughter, Lakshmi.

India has many large cities and towns, but most Indians lived in villages, without clean water or electricity. In one remote village called Champaran, in Bihar, a farmer called Shukla had heard that Mohandas wanted villagers to feel they were also part of modern India.

Shukla and his friends could not grow the food they needed because their British landlords forced them to plant indigo, which was sold to Europe as a dye for cloth. Shukla begged Mohandas to come and help them in Champaran.

As there were no roads, Mohandas and Shukla rode to Champaran on an elephant. Mohandas encouraged the villagers not to be afraid of their British landlords and to insist on growing whatever they wanted.

To the British, Mohandas was just a troublemaker, and they had him arrested. Thousands of farmers crowded around the courthouse, demanding his release. As Mohandas had not broken the law, the magistrate had to let him go. The farmers were now allowed to grow the crops they wanted.

"I only did something very ordinary", Mohandas said. "I declared that the British could not order me about in my own country."

Soon afterwards, something terrible happened in the state of Punjab, which made Mohandas realise that all of India would have to be involved in the freedom movement.

In April 1919, a British Army General ordered soldiers to fire on a crowd who had gathered peacefully to protest against the government. Hundreds of people were killed and thousands were badly wounded. The General was never punished for his cruelty, and this enraged Indians.

Mohandas travelled all over India urging everyone – students, rich businessmen, doctors, lawyers and farmers – to become peaceful soldiers in a determined effort to get the British to leave India. Many gave up their jobs and studies and went into the countryside to spread the message. All over India people refused to buy British goods, and children made bonfires of their foreign clothes and toys.

Indians loved Mohandas and called him Bapu, which means "father". He used to say that he was a Hindu, a Christian and a Muslim, and all Indians were his family. People's trust in his goodness and leadership led them to make many sacrifices in order to gain independence for their country.

One of the most unfair taxes that the British collected was on salt. As a protest, Mohandas decided not to pay the tax, but to make his own salt. Although he was now quite old, he walked 240 miles to the seashore, to get salt.

Hundreds of followers went with him, and they were cheered by villagers all along the way. When Mohandas reached the sea, he collected a pinch of salt left behind by the waves. Soon everyone was making their own salt from sea water. Sixty thousand people, all over the country, were arrested and sent to prison for breaking an unfair law.

The British did not think that Indians were ready to be in charge of their own country, so in 1931 Mohandas visited London to talk to the government. He chose to stay in the poorest area, the East End, where he was warmly welcomed. Children called him "Uncle Gandhi", and one cheeky little boy shouted, "Hey, Gandhi, where's your trousers?"

He had tea in Buckingham Palace with King George. He talked to mill workers in Lancashire about the reasons why Indians would not wear clothes imported from English factories. Even though it affected their own livelihoods, the workers understood and sympathised.

Soon after returning to India, Mohandas was once again sent to prison, together with thousands of other people who refused to obey the government. Going to jail was an expected part of their struggle for freedom from British rule, and they cheerfully allowed themselves to be arrested. Altogether Mohandas spent 2,089 days, or nearly six years of his life, in Indian prisons.

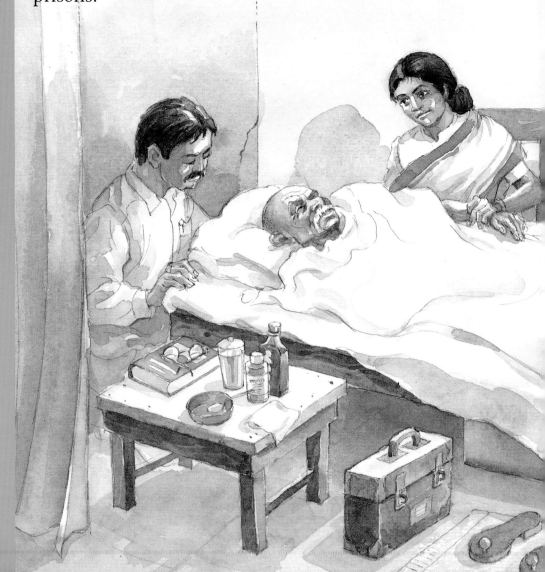

But getting rid of the British was only part of the story. Mohandas was even more interested in getting Indians to think seriously about their behaviour towards one another. Often he would fast, going without food and water to draw people's attention to the need to become kinder and more tolerant. Several times he came close to death, but he also made his countrymen think.

Although millions loved and admired Mohandas, very few were prepared to be non-violent all the time. The Indian National Congress, who were talking with the British about independence, thought that violence could sometimes be used to gain power. But Mohandas did not agree. He believed that non-violence was the only way.

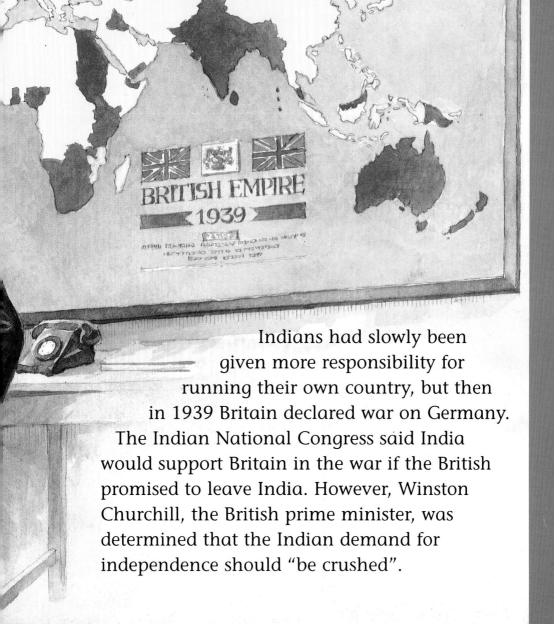

BRITISH EMPIRE
1939

Indians had slowly been given more responsibility for running their own country, but then in 1939 Britain declared war on Germany. The Indian National Congress said India would support Britain in the war if the British promised to leave India. However, Winston Churchill, the British prime minister, was determined that the Indian demand for independence should "be crushed".

After the war, the British finally realised that it was impossible to resist the Indian demand for independence. But what was an independent India going to be like? The Muslims wanted their own country. In the fear and uncertainty of what was going to happen, Muslims and Hindus started fighting. Mohandas was completely against separating Indians from one another. To him, Indians were all brothers.

Mohandas did what he had always done – he went to the most troubled area, the remote region of Noakhali, to try and teach people to love, trust and respect one another. He stayed one or two days in each village, talking to the villagers and praying for peace.

He spent four months on what he called "the most difficult and complicated mission of my life". By his example, peace reigned once again.

On August 15, 1947, India finally became free of British rule. It had been a long journey. But despite all Mohandas's efforts, India was divided into two countries, India and Pakistan. This was called Partition. Millions of Muslims crossed over the border to Pakistan, while millions of Hindus crossed into India.

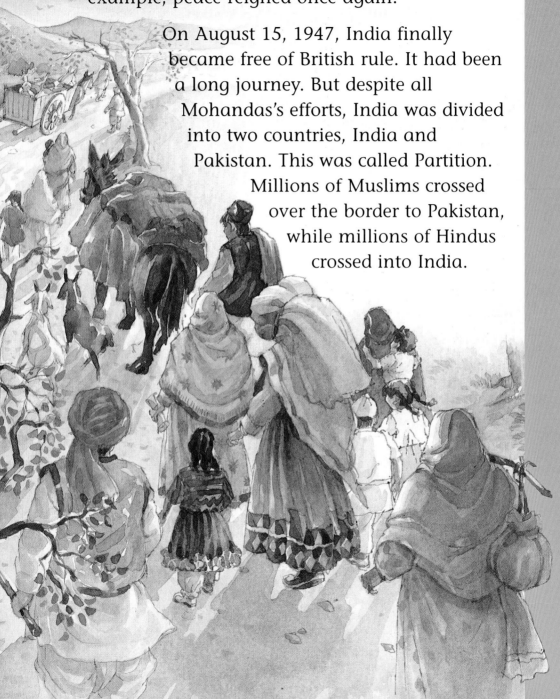

Six months after independence, Mohandas was walking to an afternoon prayer meeting at a friend's house in New Delhi. He was seventy-eight, and walked slowly, with his arms around two young female relatives. Suddenly a man came up and greeted him. As Mohandas folded his hands in *namaste*, the stranger pointed a pistol at him and fired. "Hey Rama" ("Oh God") were Mohandas's last words as he fell. He had been killed by a Hindu who could not accept his message of love and peace between Muslims and Hindus.

It was the darkest hour of India's history. "The light has gone out of our lives", grieved India's first Prime Minister, Jawaharlal Nehru. The saint whom millions loved and admired was no more.

Mohandas was dead, but his example remained. He had given people all over the world a new way of dealing with anger and hatred – the way of truth, non-violence and love for the enemy. He showed Indians how to become guardians of their own country and to be proud of their traditions.

Difficult words used in this story

dhoti A simple cotton garment worn by peasants and workers.

namaste Instead of shaking hands, many Indians greet each other by pressing their palms together and bowing their heads.

Ashram A place where a group of people live simply and work together.

Indian National Congress A group of Indians and English people that wanted Indians to be free of British rule.

Boer War A war between British and Dutch settlers in South Africa (the Dutch settlers were called Boers).

Hindus People who believe in Hinduism, one of the most ancient religions in the world. Hindus worship many gods. They believe that, when we die, we are born again on earth in a new form.

Muslims People who believe in the teachings of the prophet Mohammed. They believe that there is one God, called Allah.

Gita One of the most important holy books of the Hindu religion.

Satyagraha "Truth Force" – Gandhi's most important idea on how to fight against injustice without using violence.

independence India wanted independence from Britain. This meant that Indians wanted to choose their own government and run the country by themselves.

Index

Ashram   15
Asians   9, 11, 12
birth   4
British Empire   4, 6, 9
Champaran   16, 17
Christians   12, 20
Churchill, Winston 27
death   30
fasting   25
Hindus   5, 7, 12, 20, 28, 29, 30
independence   20, 26, 27, 28, 30
Indian National Congress 14, 26, 27
Kasturba   5, 8
London   6, 22
Muslims   12, 20, 28, 29, 30
Pakistan 29
Partition 29
prison   21, 24
Punjab   18
salt tax   20, 21
Satyagraha   12, 14
South Africa   8, 9, 10, 11, 12, 13
unfair laws   12, 13, 21
war   10, 11, 27, 28